A Bird or Two

A Story about Henri Matisse

BIJOU LE TORD

F

FRANCES LINCOLN
CHILDREN'S BOOKS

For Yannickou and Kiku
with love.

Text and illustrations
Copyright © 1999 by Bijou Le Tord
First published in the USA in 1999 by Eerdmans Books for Young Readers
An imprint of Wm. B. Eerdmans Publishing Company
255 Jefferson S.E., Grand Rapids, Michigan 49503
P.O. Box 163, Cambridge CB3 9PU U.K.

Published in Great Britain in 2008 by
Frances Lincoln Children's Books, 4 Torriano Mews,
Torriano Avenue, London NW5 2RZ
www.franceslincoln.com

British Library Cataloguing in Publication Data available on request

ISBN 978-1-84507-782-2

Set in Gill Sans.
Book design by Willem Mineur.

Printed in China

9 8 7 6 5 4 3 2 1

Author's Note

Henri Matisse made many trips to Nice (pronounced *Neece* in French) while he lived and painted in Paris. Later in his life he decided to move there permanently. By then he was already a famous artist, painter, and sculptor. He also knew colours better than almost anyone. Matisse felt very lucky to have found Nice, a place of such light and beauty.

After visiting Nice myself I decided to concentrate on the work he did while he was there. I have also included one of his paintings of dancers from an earlier period of his work because it felt important to the story of the book.

Matisse believed that his coloured paper cutouts were his best work. They reminded him of the beautiful light and colours that had intrigued him during his visit to the Island of Tahiti. He created his paper cutouts using great big scissors. Matisse began this work in his early eighties when he was ill and no longer able to walk easily or sit at his easel. Matisse never gave up his work; he loved it until the end of his life.

When I was a child my first "picture books" were the beautiful volumes of Matisse's paintings in my father's library. For me, Matisse was as familiar and as close as a member of our family, and his work is forever tied to my memories of childhood. I have kept inside me those pictures of France – its light, its colours, its great beauty. They have inspired me to create this book as a celebration of Henri Matisse and his magnificent work.

This is a partial list of museums where you can see Henri Matisse's paintings, drawings, paper cutouts, and sculptures:

UK — LONDON: The National Gallery; The Courtauld Institute of Art; Tate Modern. OXFORD: The Ashmolean Museum. CAMBRIDGE: The Fitzwilliam Museum. MANCHESTER: The Manchester Art Gallery; The Whitworth Gallery.

FRANCE — GRENOBLE: Musée de Peintures et de Sculptures. PARIS: Le Musée D' Art Moderne, Centre Georges Pompidou; Le Musée de L'Orangerie; Le Musée Picasso. NICE: Le Musée Matisse (There you can see his favorite and famous "Rococo" or Venetian chair and other furnishings from his apartment/studio at the Hotel Regina where he lived.) VENCE: La Chapelle de Vence.

CANADA — OTTAWA: The National Gallery of Canada.
SWEDEN — STOCKHOLM: Moderna Museet.
AUSTRALIA — CANBERRA: The National Gallery of Australia. SYDNEY: Art Gallery of New South Wales.
USA — NEW YORK: The Museum of Modern Art; The Metropolitan Museum. CHICAGO: The Art Institute of Chicago. BALTIMORE: The Baltimore Museum of Art: the Cone Collection. WASHINGTON DC: The National Gallery of Art. MERION: The Barnes Foundation. PITTSBURGH: The Carnegie Museum of Art. SAN FRANCISCO: The Museum of Modern Art.

When
Henri Matisse
returned
to Nice
in winter,
the brilliant sun
warmed
everything.
He looked
at the sea,
the palm trees,
and the sun
as if for
the first
time.

Because of the delicate and bright sun of Nice, Matisse's colours changed.

To his
colour
palette
he
added
the bluest
sapphire
blue
he could
imagine.
And
with it
he
painted
the
Mediterranean
Sea.

Matisse thought, "I like it here. It is a paradise. I will paint greens greener than apples, yellows more yellow than lemons."

His friends
said,
"He paints
the sunshine
every day.
He draws
everywhere,
everyone,
all the time.
He works
joyfully,
with a light
heart.
He is
enchanted."

There were no colours Matisse didn't like. He loved black and painted it just as he would any other colour.

He used it
on pure
white
paper
as a fine,
simple,
curving
line,
which he
called
an
arabesque.

He also painted it to show the cool, shady places inside his house and the light filtering from the sun outside.

Matisse
was so
delighted
with his new work
that he kept on
painting -
simply,
effortlessly.
All
his life
was in
harmony
with the way
he felt.
He wrote
to his friend
Bonnard,
also a painter,
"Long
live
painting!"

Matisse
could paint
the light
on a leaf
or the
slow-moving
branches
of palm trees
and
silvery
olive trees.

**With
just
as much
ease,
he
could
paint
dancers
in
a round
dance**

or joyful
ladies
in feathered hats
and pearls.

He also
sculpted
figures
in clay.
They too
were
cheerful
and filled
with love.

Matisse
made us
"hear"
with our
eyes
the music
he painted
in his
pictures.

He said,
"I am
strong
because
I do
what is
in my
mind."

Matisse
was
also
delicate
and
fragile.

He was
as beautiful
and
simple
as his paintings
of
mimosa flowers,
shells,
coral fish,
the sunshine,
and
a bird
or
two.